VOICES FROM AFRICA

AFRICAN CHILD

ADANU MICHAELS

ISBN 979-888606709-5

DEDICATION

The African child anthology is dedicated to all children in Africa and those who believe in building a better generation across the Globe.

Contents

Foreword

FORWARD

The book African Child Anthology is a collection of poems and short stories from around the African Continent. It is a book where several writers write to bring out the beautiful cultures and traditions of the African Nation and it extends beyond this objective to also teach the young generation the true ways of Mother Africa, to revive the fading traditions of our people and to show the whole universe the beauty and pride of the African people. Away from the cultures and traditions, some writers also dived into addressing the ill fate of structures and circumstances in some of the African countries, emphasizing on the disheartening state of the Nation and therefore pointing out possible solutions to curbing the situation.

However, aside from a few notable distinguished personalities who contributed to this anthology, majority of the contributing Authors are young African writers most of whom are students at the secondary school level and tertiary institutions. This anthology is also projected in showing to the world the potentials hidden in these young generation of African writers who have little or no opportunity to drive this big writing dream of theirs . it is no longer News that the educational standard in this new age is gradually dilapidating in most part of Africa as a result of student's poor attitude to study and learn but here, we have proof to show that we can still boast of a new age Shakespeare, new age Alexander Pope and new age Wole Soyinka. African child anthology is not just a book; it is a hope for a united Nation and a better generation

Acknowledgements

ACKNOWLEDGEMENT

I acknowledge the relentless efforts of Ukiyoto publishing house, Toronto who have given great opportunities to new and young writers in pursuit of their big dreams regardless of their statutes.

I also appreciate my great mentors; Author Tamikio L. Dooley, Barr. William Warigon and Mr. Aliu Ibrahim for their encouragement, motivations and inspirations to me.

This dream wouldn't have come to light if I had worked alone. I must appreciate my noble team of mental blinkers and all contributing Authors for this project. You have all been wonderful and great. May God bless us all to achieve more.

INTRODUCTION TO CULTURES, TRADITIONS AND PRACTICES IN AFRICA

By Adanu Michaels

INTRODUCTION TO CULTURES, TRADITIONS AND PRACTICES IN AFRICA

African Tradition is expressed through many different art forms, such as music, dance, art, sculpture and beadwork. These traditions are deeply ingrained into the whole African culture. Many African languages are "tone languages," meaning that pitch level determines meaning.

Oral Tradition

Oral tradition is very important in African culture, as it insures the passage of cultural practices from one generation to another.

LISTENING TRADITION

Listening is an equally important skill, which has been perfected by the traditional oral practices. Numerous songs and dances have been transmitted by word of mouth.

Music and Poetry in African Traditions

Naturally, singing is very important to the African society because the melody and rhythm follow the intonation of the song text. The songs are often sung in call-and-response form. In West Africa, a griot is a praise singer or poet who possesses a repository of oral tradition passed down from generation to generation. They must know the traditional songs and must also be able to improvise songs about current events and chance incidents.

Music is a form of communication and it plays a functional role in African society. Songs accompany marriage, birth, rites of passage, hunting and even political activities. Music is often used in different African cultures to ward off evil spirits and to pay respects to good spirits, the dead and ancestors. Although the musical styles and instruments vary from region to region, there are some common forms of musical expression. The most significant instrument in African music is the African drum. It expresses the mood of the people and evokes emotion. The beat of the African drum is the "heartbeat of the community" and its rhythm is what holds the dancers together.

Dance is an integral part of the African culture, and it utilizes symbolic gestures, masks, costumes, body painting and props to communicate. The dance movements can be simple or complex with intricate actions including fast rotation, ripples of the body and contraction and release. Dance is used to express emotion, whether joyful or sorrowful and it is not limited to just the dancers. Often spectators will be encouraged to join in.

Traditional African Masks

The African masks that are used in dances have religious, ceremonial and functional origins. The artist who carves the mask will ceremonially purify himself and offer prayers to his ancestors for guidance before he begins the actual carving of the mask. The African mask represents a spirit and it is believed that the spirit possesses the dancer as they wear the mask. The chosen dancer goes into a trance-like state in order to receive guidance and wisdom from the ancestors. The dancer will utter and moan the messages received and a wise man who accompanies the dancer, will translate the message.

Art

Although music and dance are extremely important African traditions and are very common forms of communication, many African people express themselves in other art forms as well.

Zulu woman wearing intricate bead work only her husband would understand. The Zulu people are well known for their intricate beadwork. The colour of each bead carries a specific meaning. The beads have been used to carry messages known as "ucu," a Zulu term loosely translated as “love letters”. It is an African tradition for young girls to send a boy a beaded bracelet of different colours. The boy will court her for a while and at the appropriate time; he will ask her the meaning of the beads.

Art and sculpture are prevalent in African culture, and the most common themes depict a couple, a woman and child, a male with a weapon or animal, or a “stranger.” Couples are usually freestanding figures of the same size, representing the importance of “two as one.” A male and female couple in African art usually depicts strength and honour rather than love and intimacy, as it is uncommon for African men and women to publicly display their affection.

A mother and child couple can represent “mother earth” and her people or the strong bond between mother and child while the male figure with a weapon or animal, represent honour to departed ancestors. African men are often honoured in warfare and there is a great emphasis on weaponry in African art, as it depicts survival and power. When the stranger is represented in African art, it usually depicts someone from a foreign country or tribe that is not welcomed.

LIVING WITH THEIR MOTHERS

In the **Gio tribe** in Ivory Coast, children never live with their fathers. The women of the tribe have their own houses (typically small huts), where they live with their children until the children are old enough to move out.

SONS ARE RAISED BY UNCLES

In the Northern Angolan; **Songo tribe**, when male children reach the age 5 or 6 years, they are sent to live with their uncles on the mother's side. This is because, in their society, chiefs inherit their titles and positions through matrilineal lines.

PRESERVING WILD ANIMALS

The **Massai** people of Kenya and Tanzania are averse to killing wild animals. They freely keep cattle and livestock, but wild animals are left untouched. This is largely because they consider these wild animals clan members, and each clan is associated with a specific species which they often keep close to them and treat as a clan member.

BEATING THE SUITOR

In the **Fulani tribe** in West Africa, the custom of beating the suitor is followed as part of the **Sharo** tradition. The custom is followed when two men are vying for the same woman. To determine the eventual suitor of the woman, the men are asked to compete for the hand of the woman by beating themselves up. The man, who is able to take the beating while showing the least or no sign of pain, can take the woman as a wife. The people of the tribe might not practice the tradition as strictly as they once did, but there are still some parts of the tribe that practice it to the letter.

AFRICAN CULTURES AND TRADITIONS

The courtship dance of the Wodaabe

Birds do it. Bees do it. We're talking, of course, about a courtship dance. In the **Wodaabe tribe of Niger**, the human mating ritual takes a page from nature's book. The **Guérewol** is an annual ritual and competition that sees young men dress up in elaborate ornamentation and traditional face paint and gather in lines to dance and sing. The goal? To get the attention of one of the judges – a marriageable young woman. In this particular tribe, the male beauty ideal is all about bright eyes and teeth, so men will often roll their eyes and bare their teeth to show off their sex appeal

The lip plates of the Mursi

The Mursi tribe of Ethiopia is one of the last tribes in Africa where it's the norm for women to wear large pottery or wooden plates in their lower lips. When a **Mursi** girl reaches the age of 15 or 16, her lower lip is cut by her mother or another older woman in the settlement. The cut is held open by a wooden plug for about three months while it heals. **Mursi** members are rather egalitarian – girls are never forced to have their lip pierced; it's a totally personal choice. (Of course, 16 is the prime age for peer pressure no matter your culture, and this is often the reason girls opt for the lip plate.)

The bull jumping of the Hamar

Ethiopia's Hamar tribe (also known as the Hamer tribe), made up mostly of pastoralists who respect and treasure their cattle, has a rather athletic initiation ritual. Forget cow tipping – this tradition is all about the art of bull jumping. Bull jumping is a three-day rite of passage that all boys must partake in, and it's extremely important for the dignity of both the initiate and his family. The initiate must walk over 15 castrated bulls that have been rubbed in dung to make their backs slippery (and the task that much tougher). If he fails, he'll have to wait a whole year to try again and if he succeeds it means he's ready to marry a girl of his parents' choosing, and to raise his own children and cattle.

The red ochre of the Himba

The women of this iconic **Namibian tribe** are known for their beautiful, red-tinged skin and hair. The reason for the rich colour? A homemade paste of butter, fat and red ochre known as ***otjize***. Girls in the tribe start using ***otjize*** as soon as they're old enough to care for their own hygiene. There has long been speculation around exact origins of the practice, with many people claiming it acts as sun protection or insect repellent. But the **Himba** tribe says it's purely for aesthetic reasons – effectively a traditional make-up they apply every morning in the same way we'd slap on a lick of mascara and lipstick.

The spitting of the Maasai

The Maasai people of Kenya and Northern Tanzania view spitting as a form of blessing and a sign of respect. Tribes people use spitting to greet or say goodbye to friends clinch a bargain or to wish someone good luck. Two friends greeting each other will spit in their palms before shaking hands. When a baby is born, family members will spit on the child to wish him or her long life and good luck. Spitting is also customary on a daughter's wedding day, where her father will spit on her forehead to wish her a blessed union.

The healing dance of the San

Of all the tribal traditions, this one is arguably the most magical. For the **San people of South Africa,Namibia, Botswana and Angola,** dance is considered a sacred power. One of their most integral tribal traditions is the trance dance (also known as the healing dance). The whole community comes together around a fire for several hours or even an entire night, led by healers and elders. The healers dance around the fire, chant and hyperventilate until they induce a powerful trance-like state. In this state, they are granted access to the spirit world (and are often able to walk over fire). The San healers aren't just doing this to cure physical illnesses in their community – they also attempt to expel what they call "star sickness", a force that causes jealousy, anger and arguments.

The wedding ceremony of the Ndebele

The Ndebele wedding ceremony is all about the bride – and her attire puts western white dresses to shame. This, in most part, is thanks to her future mother-in-law and the prettiest of all the tribal traditions. The groom's mother creates a ***Jocolo*** for the bride – an apron made of goatskin and decorated with gorgeous, colourful beads. The ***Jocolo*** is worn by all married women at the wedding ceremony, and is representative of a mother surrounded by children. On their wedding day, the groom performs a ceremony in honour of his new wife, giving her thanks and credit for everything she's done for him in their time together.

POETRY

THE AFRICAN CHILD

By EZENWAJIAKU PEARL

A – Africa – The world's best continent. Africa is

F – Fruitfully blessed with various

R – Regions, races, radically virtuous humans. We are

I – Intelligent, powerful, truthful also

C – Courageous, unlimited personalities

A – Always humble to the core. We are

N – Nations combined and filled with hospitable personalities.

C – Combined together we are unstoppable and united

H – Honest and truthful to ourselves no matter what

I – In all cases we remain Africa

L – Leaders that leave a legacy behind yet

D – Domineering in all our endeavors.

We are Africa

I am an African child

I belong to the African party where values are tightly held

Not much entertainment is held there

But I learnt that good people actually exist

They exist within me, my African home and society

With Africa my continent filled with generations

That I would always and never cease to admire

A party that will always shield me in its unending love and eternal bond

I am an African child

And in the African party

All I see and think of as at now is

Relatively explained as a set of nations celebrating victory

All I feel in this bond is love

That includes contacts of the world

Nations that uphold values and still age in grace

Nations that love and still care in this modern age.

I am an African child with the Africa beauty

I am a black child and still so proud

Proud of the richness of my culture

Proud of the love I see around me

Proud of my color because black is bold

It is not dark

It is gold I love my Africa.

We uphold value, love education as we should and still express our love

I am one African that would always salute Africa and its founding fathers

I hail my founding fathers

Nelson Mandela of South Africa

Nnamdi Azikiwe of Nigeria

Tafawa Balewa of Nigeria

Kwame Nkrumah of Ghana

Obafemi Awolowo of Nigeria

I am the African child who has the privilege of sitting under the moonlight listening to my grandpa with rich stories from our rich culture

Raced with tires and swam in the rivers with my fellow kids.

Unfortunately this does not happen in the western world

But as the days progresses from the visiting of the sun to my days of living long

I have always longed to be a member of this party. The African party.

I am an African child from an African home with an African mom

Who would always boil with anger whenever I deviate from family culture

Who would always threaten to send me to an early grave

If I fall short of my value or norms, by coming home with pregnancy without marriage nor husband

I have Africa to hold my back whenever

That is Africa my Africa.

Even in this party of mine

I have little or no knowledge of my founding fathers and how they are celebrated

I want to pray and also hope that little lesson will be provided with little differences from what mom has taught me

I will be consistent at celebrating Africa even in a million years to come

I am still grateful to Africa

I am still proud to be an African child

I enjoy the African party where our presentations are incomparable and spirituality is a man's core business.

Thank you Africa for making me your own.

THE GIRL CHILD

By EZENWAJIAKU PEARL

She is a mystical creature said to have existed long ago.

She works under the scorching sun to hit a target

And get burnt, yet her ashes would form again and will re-incarnate

She would fight like never before

She who fights with fire and is not scared of burning

Because she is the phoenix, the mighty one

She knows she is born to live once, born to leave a legacy behind

A warrior yet a survivor, hard yet kind

She is as hard as a rock.

She is a flower that blooms in the winter

Truthfully honest to herself without minding her awkward colour

She stands tall racing the tides because she is heavenly and God sent

And now the hour has come

She let the breeze take her petals on a wild tour

A tour that will bring forth life

To all those who viewed her as a disgrace

For she is flawless in beauty yet so tender at heart

She is powerful, fearless and above all a person who sacrificed all to become all.

But why do I say this?

I say so because she and she alone is the girl child

The female gender

Is every agenda

Made to remember

Every mild flower.

FANTASY

By EZENWAJIAKU PEARL

I woke up to my dream, a wonderful one

Bought a limousine

Hanging with Jana Ietrasini

I was in my mansion

Chilling in my cushion

Eating marrying

Drinking jollying

Enjoying laps, wings and fat

Watching moves with my pals

As if it was all fake

I heard my name

Waking up to the harsh realities of life

Realizing it was all a lie

Waking up drooling with my book and pen.

My mum staring at me so concerned

So I gave her the gist

Not missing a bit

So I picked up my pen

Writing my fantasy with tears in my eyes

Wondering why the world is made up of lies

Today, I write out my dreams with beams

For they are mine,

My fantasy.

AFRAID

By EZENWAJIAKU PEARL

Stand strong when life changes

Stand strong through the ups and downs

Stand strong because we all know that God is in control

Afraid means scared

Scared people don't win

Winners don't develop cold feet

They only develop bold and positive vibes

So why should we be scared

When we should be feared

Among our equals

No one can top us

So why then should be afraid.

When we have faced hardship of any

Meanwhile a country is facing a possible third term saga

There is no bread on our table

And Israelites got heavenly manner

We are not afraid we are able

And no matter what, we press harder

Why then should we be afraid when we battled with death

Deterioration is the order of the day in citizen's health

Afraid is not a successful trail

It is a low esteemed rail.

DEPRESSED

By EZENWAJIAKU PEARL

You scream in pain and claim its okay

Lest it's not, it will always be tough

You are lifting weights saying it pays

Payment of what, payment without works

You are not alone, don't run from home.

You are depressed, no offence, you are oppressed

You conceal the pain believe me you won't gain

You want liberty; there is no liberty from puberty

You want to run from home, you want to be free

Wait a minute, ask yourself

Do I believe in myself?

You want to be rich, it's not a flinch

We are dust, we shall rust

We are ashes and ashes we shall return

In that same turn, you can't outrun the race you need to overcome.

You are thinking, wondering what they would say

You are already on your way

You are wallowing in abject poverty

Complaining who will explain to me

Not insult me but instruct and construct me.

Know that is a matter of time

You are hurting but it's all part of life

You are not better of running

The best decision is to let it out

Just hug everyone and start rejoicing

Soon they will say darling

You will never be alone, you are always

Welcome at home.

OH! YOU GENTLE PEACE

By Babangida B. Shira

Your name sounds peace

Peace, by which humans appease

For your gems

I'm word-less, by all ways

Oh, you gentle peace, humanity.

Be not a coryphaeus of cruelty,

Be not in the hands of miser.

Be a damsel of all societal tars

We're in paucity of your meek

Come here, gaze out to seek

Mankind turns hunters: killing,

Tethering, prejudicing--hamming

The smother protuberant values

Humanity seek the silk in norms

Sorry here, we chant. Oh you the

Sear of heart's beings! Agape the

Gape of lives' overture sounds of

You, oh my beloved humanity

Let you not sink us in this glued-globe, of vampires, of humiliated globe.

Oh peace! Rescue the skirts, the toys and the caps

To tilt the undeveloped democracy

Out of our heads.

A LETTER TO NIGERIAN GOVERNMENT

By Babangida B. Shira

Harbinger rings:

Oh! Earth note,

Those ants breed,

Corn scarce behind;

Hand jams, space boring

Huge smirking, hefty smiling-

Music stopped, ravels dance.

Youths stuff:

Zillions institutions vomit,

From both head and legs.

Foot suffuse the land

While shoes burned!

Dull plan class the Nation orifices

Even not the peep-point to breath.

Land's wall:

Surmising, Tom to speak good

Jerry most march his footsteps.

Ovation not for poor masses but,

Self curiosity is the best.

Don't think a repercussion of-

Ravenous Lion roam for its aims;

In stadium there it landed, will you escape?

Keep covetous behind.

Tilt the selfish and work,

The lacks of lack install!

Many minds' decide wrong that make:

Kidnappings to dance,

Burglary to speak,

Robbery to breath,

Terrorism over powered.

Oh! Job sorry,

The predilection of each one.

Eagerness of graduated persons,

To have it in each one's room;

In highest pride of its merit

In lowest hands you hold.

Let work ahead the needs.

Iron's and rubbers' advice use,

So, welfare unlocks, poverty locks.

Cry and wail at once

We should relief from constant speech.

The land will hug smile to the infinity.

SWINGER

By Babangida B. Shira

To and fro

To and fro

Life swings

Swing tricks

Time goes

Going rapids

Human oblivion

Oblivion keeps

Out of relief

Reels around

Smile in pain

Pain of tyrant

Laugh in starve

Starved by whom?

Plethora of food

Food for fewer

Fewer of thugs

Thug more innocents

AREWA MOON

By William Warigon

My sweet Arewa moon

I long to see you soon

Long have I sojourned in these harsh plains

That detests my sunburned skin and the rains

Of hate pelt at me with ferocious fires

Arewa moon, you swirl in my desires

These cold nights are lonely

Strangers I see; they're horny

With the living blood lust of the vilest beast

They mince my meat and have me for feast.

My dry ears long to be wetted by your music

The distant echoes of your drums homesick

Me beyond measure. I want to hear ululations

Of the sweet women I had in diverse relations.

Let me hold harmattan and kiss her dry lips.

I want my hair whitened by her hazy hue.

Blurring but yet the winds lolls upon her hips

And make the morning fires taker of blue.

To Arewa bound train I must train my mind.

The green grasses beckon. The gold mine

Will wait till I till the memories from the past

Under Arewa moon, I shall find peace at last

THE FATE OF RIVER BORN CHILD

By William Warigon

The vile villagers cooked coldest rumour

Of a corrugated take of this beautiful child

That she's a river child that brought tumour

To the prevailing peace. And the child is mild

And the most beautiful in the village.

Her beauty scared the inhabitants.

Their eyes never be-held in any age

Such luciferous beauty even on infants.

The myth festered and the baby was to die

By offering sacrifice to the river goddess.

Her mother cried but her father stoutly deny

To assuage the whims of the acrimonious.

The false gods and their perpendicular fires

Hide behind the minds of the ignorant

To batter new dreams for capricious desires.

Fate forces herself and favour she'd grant.

The river born child was saved,

Caravels transpierced from coast to coast

In the Africa with strange graved

Beliefs on oblivion's shore are insipid boast.

WE WERE ONCE DISCIPLINED

By William Warigon

Once upon a time

We wedged war against indiscipline

That trying time

The act of discipline was the 'In' thing

Even embryos stopped kicking their mothers

For fear of sadist soldiers' boots kicking

To drink water, prayers were uttered in altars

To smile, permission was needed via queuing

The fleeing Andrews returned

From fancy foreign sojourn

Corruption was truly sunburned

Giant of Africa blowing a horn

Essential commodities flooded markets

Coins were used to pay dowry

Decent ways were everyone's parapets

Governance had transparency

So, I ask, confused as a drunk

"What went wrong?"

How education could have us dunk

In quagmire that's pong?

A tangibly tall answer awaits me, I know.

The apropos of the answer

Comes when in heavenly chateau I bow

And to divine joy I surrender

AFRICA'S AFFLICTION AMELIORATED

By William Warigon

Songs from sweet Sudan's lips

Spurned us to rejoice

There's progress coming in heaps

Men are no longer boys

Yesterday's inertia is gone

Despotic tendencies are now taboo

The voice of the people's turned

From subservience to assertive, anew

The wars that had ravaged our motherland

Branding on our tired faces dried blood

From the excess of the militia's vile hand

Had finally opened our eyes in a ballad

Of determination to take our future

Into our open arms

How come xenophobia is a fixture?

Many men are apt and up in arms

Fighting debuting diseases

While insurgents destroying farms

Fanning embers of hunger

Despots sit tight on thrones they stole

Wearing gowns of corruption with impunity

Africa, you are not cursed to stay stale

Come, fight for progress and peace in unity

MY BENUE

By Matthew Edeh Sunday

I was named Benue

Born to the north

Yet to the north I belong not

So I reside in her center.

I am not deep in hustle

My quest is to solve the howling of stomach puzzle

My basket is never empty

Even when I feed millions of mouth.

I am a tree with many varieties of fruits

Wild and meek

My son's are industrious like an ant

My daughter's are melanin in physique.

I am Benue

Adorned with culture

Endorsed by nature

Recognized for passion in pleasure.

My land is fertile

I harbour the element that gives life

My face is rough and un-kept

But I believe in the future so I hope.

AKWA IBOM

By Matthew Edeh Sunday

She's my Canaan land

Because she's the land of promise.

Her sons are brave and mighty like the guardian of Eden

Her daughters sparkle like the goddess of beauty.

Let the eyes that see ekpo run

And let the belly that smells "editan" dance.

We don't pay too much homage to the soil

But Abasi have never let our sweat to spoil.

Come gather around

"Asian Ubo Ikpa" and swing your waist to the drumbeat of "mbopo"

Swift your feet with the magic of "asian mbre iban"

Let your charms attracts the sight of your bond.

We are endowed with the apparel of culture

Our breathe stinks with hospitality

The key to knowledge lives within our conformity

Culture is our heritage

She is our identity.

MAKURDIAN

By Matthew Edeh Sunday

Far away with pride

She planted her huts

Above the hills

Where the guts of the river danced in-between her fills

Stronger and better she grew and exists

Like the ancient city of Greek

She has seen many faces of the sun.

She is the Knot of the North

So sitting on her fence isn't her fault

She sings melodies of songs that drag the echoes of bellies to halt

Her arms are spread open to accommodate

Like a forest

She's blessed for rest.

We are proud of you mother of old

The woman with the basket of foods

Let not the tempest by your children change your mood

For their veins are still flowing with your blood.

MAMA AFRICA

By Matthew Edeh Sunday

Chinmamanda called her Africanna

She's the heartbeat of the Terra

Enriched with natural endowment

Home of all segments

Let's go and visit her daughters

Through the breathe of South Africa

To behold the smiles of friendly faces

The mosaic of cultures and cuisines

With spring wildflower bloom at Goegap Nature Reserve Namaqualand

Oh hail pretty South Africa

With landscapes made up of valleys, mountains, forests, deserts, coastlines

And grassy savannahs that are breath-taking in their picturesque scale.

Take a break at the unclasp of Kenya

To glimpse at the smiling island of Mombasa

The sheer beauty of wildlife and amazing safaris

Coastal sunsets where titanic peak it stand.

Watch over the treaties of Ghana

Where bellies rejoices at the sight of banku

Her smallness speaks strength and love

Home of great heroes and pioneers.

When you get to the giant of Africa

A land for none but all

A place where millions of tongue gather

A place where passing though the bone to get meat matters

You will not deny the pride of Africa?

After sweeping through the homes of Nigeria

She's one with thirty six

Divided in stand but united in fall

Then will you praise Mama Africa.

THE OLD BRIDGE

By Matthew Edeh Sunday

I remember the old trail

When we learnt from the elder's teeth

When we never knew the four walls of a school.

I remember the old trail

When at twenty we still act as kids

Moonlight dance and chants

Our ears were opened for the tell of tales.

I remember the old trail

When though we were clever

Our brains eye only the bush

Chasing animals

Gathering fruits and roots.

I remember the old trail

When love was pure and genuine

When fist boast in the abundance of their field

When heroes on the battle were known.

Sweet ancient memories we knew

From you we became new

We are gone from you

To another master we hew.

A POET'S LIFE.

By Ruth Koech

Looking at me

You may think

Think that my bed is made of roses

Not knowing how thorny it is

To a point I think twice before lying down on it

In order to avoid getting pricked.

I‘m known to be cheerful

You may think I lead the cheering squad

My pen is meant to deceive

Fake my emotions

Having unseen tears

While I’m dying from within.

I‘m known to be a player

Yet I play on ball games

Neither do I toss ladies like chips

Loneliness clouds my world

As emptiness fills my soul

While accusations rain on me.

Yes I'm a poet

Making others happy is my obligation

Relieving others from their misfortune is my job

But I'm forgotten and seen as dirt

They curse me aside

Knowing I'm not a robot and I got feelings.

Being a poet is a journey

A journey full of pain

I walk bare footed on hot rocks

Some cut through my flesh

Whether I bleed or not, no one cares

Like a lone wolf I am meant to journey by myself!

IN LOVE

By Ruth Koech

I'm Myles

They call me the Masterpiece

I spit to impress

As I inspire

Leaving them highly elevated

Though not in a toxic way.

I'm spitting

Not to impress you

But to woo you

As I play with words

I don't intend to play with your feelings

I want to keep it real and true.

Your smile, damn your smile!

It leaves me confused,

Though I'm not a fresher,

I'll do the impossible,

I mean the impossible,

To ensure you always wear that smile.

Ms pretty, yes you..

Take my heart,

Let's board into love,

I'm the ticket you need,

Don't shred me like a paper,

Like a stain full dirt, I'm stuck on you.

THE CURRENT WORLD

By Ruth Koech

A different world we're living in...

Mass confusion... increasing sin.

Time for change...to rearrange.

To go now back to God again

Uncertainty grows and no one knows...

What comes next or where this goes...

Ever strange kinds of danger.

The future only our God knows.

It seems unreal... can you feel...

That growing to stop and kneel?

There's a war...a battle for....

The soul this world seek to steal.

Regardless why, when all men die.

To almighty God they cry,

Some with fear that God draws near....

Some relieved that they believed..

The gospel message all men hear.

Long foretold Days of old

The love of many now grows cold,

We know somehow the time is now...

To live in faith becoming bold.

To do what we've rarely done..

Proclaim to men what he has done.

Reaching out be free from doubt,

Upon that cross this war was worn!

In faith obey and fully trust...

Leaving sin behind in dust,

In power preach to the lost now reach..

What man creates will someday rust.

What God foretold has come to pass...

Soon he shall return at last,

The time is now...Christ showed us how.

Let that stubborn sin become your past.

Glorify the God who is.

Who suffered and died to make us his...

Commit... begin by seeking him...

Become the one by faith that lives!

THE LIFE

By Ruth Koech

The lie it's okay,

Saying okay is like ABC,

So easy, but deep in,

It's too hard to spell the ABC out.

Disguising is at its best,

The lie it's okay,

It isn't,

Just to cover sorrows,

And trying to keep moving.

It's not easy, pain and confusion,

Still stand for,

Emotions fighting for dominance,

The lie it's okay,

For yes it's okay, I say

But it isn't super clarified.

I am the only being,

Who knows what's happening in me,

The multitude will never understand,

It burns in me,

Like the midnight oil.

No one will ever get my case,

The lie it's okay,

Twill still stand,

Yes it's still okay,

No one will ever get it

MONSTER

By Ruth Koech

It flooded and forth an ocean originated

Who knew it would spread this far?

On my own opinion when I first saw it on the headlines

Took it as a pass by thing

Two weeks later headlines notify

Emergence of a dreadful virus

Voices all roared

One meter distance

Interaction has deteriorated

Special and heartfelt greetings have gone down to the sand

The sweet meaningful contact elapsed

We have run out of negotiation skills

Honeymoons and dates are called off

Bear hugs and smooth kisses

Blown away by the wind they have been

Who knew we would come to this?

Coughs and sneezes are the engine Coughers

Forth leading to social distancing

Ignore the rule then take the risk

For infectious the virus is, keep social distance

AFRICA

By Precious Lawrence

Africa, as old as time itself

Hence the mother of continents

Thirty percent of the earth's mineral resides in her domain

Rich fertiled brown soil

Natural resources such as gold and oil

Acres of green fields

Lands with so much to yield

The tropical rainforest that houses beautiful birds that chirps at the wee hours of the morning

To the beautiful deserts and sand dunes

Africa, where you find the hills, valleys from the beautiful mountains to the glorious waterfalls

Beautiful sights as the sunsets.

Home of wildlife, from the lion In the Savannah

To the jaguar In the rainforest and the subtle snake in the deserts.

Africa, her daughters are her pride

Ranging from slim and slender

To thick and curvy with her thick kinky hair

Confident in her own skin be it brown or fair

She's phenomenal and resilient

Passionate in pursuit of her dreams and aspirations.

She multitasks, she's in the boardroom, kitchen she's a mother and a wife

She's amenable and accommodating

She wears different hats effortlessly.

Africa oh her son she prides herself in

Strongly built adapting to every climate change

Cold, dry or hot

The strength of thousands resides in him

Standing tall and firm even in the face of challenges

The husband to the wife, father to the children and leader at work.

Africa the smoke that thunders

The voice in the mountains

Home to nations

Home to thousands of tongues

Full of hospitality and kindness

United even in diversities

Africa a home for all.

THE INDEPENDENCE DAY

By Victor Chinazaekpere

A poem dedicated to Nigeria in their Independence Day.

I write to my nation.

It all started with from a journey of miles

To serve our fatherland

In love and in strength and faith

Regardless of the corruption in the land

Yet we fought to uphold the justice of our nation

Crimes and threats hovering all over the land,

Yet, we fought as heroes past,

Fire burning all over our bodies,

Yet, we fought to uphold the nation

Chanting our national anthem,

Yet we were burnt up to death

Moving forward with the nation's flag,

Yet we endured the pain

Handing over the Barton and the flag to the men ahead

Yet we maintained our track

Bullets flying all over the sky

Killing and slaughtering our men of war

Yet, we kept on paying the price

Oh, with bullets in our bodies, we sing

Arise o compatriots

Nigeria's calls obey.

To serve our fatherland

With love and strength and faith

The labor of our heroes past

Shall never be in vain

To serve with heart and might

One nation bound in freedom, peace and unity

They tried to restrict us but we cried out ?

I pledge to Nigeria my country

To be faithful, loyal and honest

To serve Nigeria with all my strength

To defend her unity

And uphold thy honor and glory

So help us Lord

The dignity of our nation was established by the price we paid

Fighting to eliminate crimes and corruption in our land

But what do we get in return???

BRUTALITY!

BRUTALITY!!

BRUTALITY!!!

Exhibited by our leaders now!

Killing and shading the bloods of our children we raised

Practicing Terrorism and they call it tribalism

Oh, our souls and spirit are in tears

Crying "PEACE AND UNITY" please be restored to the land we raised, in this INDEPENDENCE DAY BEING 1st of October...

E HEROES ERA

By Victor Chinazaekpere

Once we sat as one, as children we were,

Under the mango tree in the mid night hour,

Surrounded by peace and power

Corruption was not found in that our era

For we were in the heroes era,

Peace and unity was all we see and sing

Love and strength was the bond that kept us living

Oh! Africa was the pride of the world

Because criminology was never treated as tribology

But when the hero's era was over, I began to write in anthology,

Reminding Africa her pride and glory

Reminding her of our oath to defend the heroes past

Oh Africa, the beauty of all the nations,

You shall be well again, if only u remember your ancient history.

AFRICA MY LAND

By Victor Chinazaekpere

I am from a land, the land of brave men,

Where dark men are born, born of expectations

Oh black is your beauty, the beauty among all creation

Giving birth to many nations,

Nations full of Brave men

NIGERIA you raised, the home of hard work

GHANA you raised, the home of Justice

You bear in you the melodious language, compare not to others

IGBO, HAUSA AND YORUBA, The three major ethnic groups of Nigeria

Which are your pride and your manpower

But now, the drum bit have changed

An enemy has come into the land,

Mohammed have become armed robbers we have

Oh Africa, where is thy beauty?!

Where is thy pride?

AFRICA

By Victor Chinazaekpere

I once saw a dark maiden sitting on the roadside, sad and lonely

With tears flowing from her eyes

Oh, I sought to know

Oh beautiful damsel, why sited alone on the roadside, with tears flowing from your eyes?

'I am neither crying nor alone' she said

I am alive, Happy and joyous. Though my children have abandoned me and my enemies have become my help mates

'My sons being killed by my siblings and my siblings living a gloomy life in all their existence'

Oh, let me cry in peace, the tears of victory ?

For Africa shall be great again

Peace shall be restored again

For a new phase shall emerge, brighter than the sky of the earth

Flowing than the oceans of the earth and burning than the volcano of the earth

Regardless of my condition, yet I shall be well again

I weep ? with my ears but rejoice with my heart for Africa shall be well again.

THE ROOT OF THE UNKNOWN GUN MEN

By Victor Chinazaekpere

When we spoke gently

They listened not to our voices with laughter

Sad complaining of voice of Berger

They abandoned us to stagger

When we cried of our roughly torments

Ever increasing from the start of things

They watched our large mouths hunger

And shaped off the laughter of our children

Who will render to help us?

We clamoured and murmured

They blocked ear to our pitiful tears

Which grows in us like a tumor in the white depth of our plaintive throats

Our dead bodies have come up with the dead buried in the grave

But our soul cries out for vengeance

For we are fathers and mothers buried in years back

For we are brothers and sisters buried in years

We cried to government with our clumsy voices

But they were deaf to our cries

They destroyed our hope

They destroyed our markets

And left the promises hanged on the air

Because of them, we died

Because of them, we left the earth

Leaving our cries on the air

On the water and on the Land so that our sons will hear and trace

They have traced it and have chosen to adhere to our cries

To avenge and to pay pack

Our sons are the UNKNOWN GUN MEN

Who chose to wipe our tears

For the happiness of their generation

They watched us suffered when they were small

They depended on the promises of the government which were left unfulfilled

They watched they parents died because of the unfulfilled promise

Now they have chosen to avenge back in satisfaction of our hearts and minds

But who restore the nation back to peace?

Men now play out of role

In breaking the rules

Set by our heroes past

Oh

We cry for peace of heart in our nation

MY VILLAGE ABOUT THIS TIME

BY OLETU OGHENENYORE CORNELIUS

And it is September, the climax

Of the festival of the water gods.

Alluring fishes swam from the city,

Circling the village pond as the rain

Speak heavily, for several days.

I lay, not sleeping back home,

Papa won't allow us near the square

Spirits rent human bodies to live in

So he believes at these times.

Then, the thunder will laugh loudly,

Lightening soon follow its footsteps

Like sheep to the abattoir, using the

Judas' goat, taking photos along.

Photos only those in heaven can flick through.

Am sure during these feasts,

The gods are in deep romance,

Procreating a fruitful season ahead.

Natives happily tie ogélé* to do

The ogbö-urié† dance at the riverbank

Spoon feeding the water gods with gifts

Brought in doxology for the past season.

Senseless city dwellers think the

Endless rituals in our village are

Useless, religion mouth is so wide.

Yet to attend one anyway because of Papa

But Grandpa thinks otherwise.

With new numbers on me, yearly,

I will find out, someday, for myself.

Note:

*Ogélé is a traditional wear of natives in Southern Nigeria during events or festivities.

†Ogbö-urié is a marine festival associated with the Urhobo indigenes of Delta Nigeria.

THE BEAUTY OF YESTERDAY

BY OLETU OGHENENYORE CORNELIUS

I would sit on our step, and watch time fly

After school hours, each day after homework.

The other children fly kites, the girls do leg dance happily,

A familiar scene I'm used to but wasn't allowed to join.

Grandma lost her teeth long ago, I didn't ask how.

Grandpa's head was never a chimney like the others.

Their fingers do a peace sign over their mouth,

But backwards, burning cigarette, stick after stick,

I wonder how tobacco tastes.

Have they peace within their soul?

What about the chest pain and lung aches?

Same thing youths now face.

Dad fell in love with that white man Book, he never

Took a second wife, but mom, the God Book won't allow it.

He barricades our feet off the festival path, sad but glad

That Book has been my map since then.

It was not distasting, we had angelic neighbours then.

My child can't comprehend my stories,

How can ten naira cooked meals for a family of ten?

And lasting many days afterwards? He asks repeatedly.

My eyes did see the beauty of yesterday, beautiful things

What we don't today see?

That was before Grandma died. Then grandpa,

Ten years later. That was ten years before the Covid-nineteen.

A lot has changed since I cross teen.

I can tell, son, trust me, I can tell.

TODAY WAS NOT YESTERDAY

BY OLETU OGHENENYORE CORNELIUS

Yesterday's torch flicker on my mind,

I stood, doing my tie,

Remembering my goldmine fantasy.

Oh mirror boy I smiled, so happy for sure

After a dry harmattan spell that took me donkey years to weigh down.

I was year six, or seven then,

Over twenty years ago.

We would roast corn in its season

Or yams in oil dip, or sauce under the moonlight

Listening to tales and wisdom pearls.

The land was green when the southern rain call

We would party under its tear, make sure Mama was away.

Hello, Mayday! Shrrrrrriiii... Kriii...

Hello... Hello... Over, can you read me.

That's what we hear today, as human birds keep falling from the sky.

The African children once living in serenity

Has learnt wild dialects.

Cows disturb their memory for learning,

Now they hate school?

Farms in limbo.

The iron bamboo abduct his father, ransom cost

He became an orphan.

Hands-on the head by day

Watch moon at night, not for tales

But writing his own story, the hard way.

I tap his back,

Son, let's go to better land

It exists but in my head.

I still hadn't forgotten my goldmine fantasy.

As I knot my tie, ready for work

I remember today was not yesterday.

MY AFRICAN HERITAGE

By Wilfred Ntui

My Africa! My heritage!

My culture! My pride,

My treasure! My assurance

The home of great heroes,

The home of gold and silvers,

The bedrock of the world's natural resources.

The home of great festive, mostly the

Calabar carnival, a festival beautify by diversity of cultures

Calling people from far and near to taste the beauty and splendor of Africa.

Oh Africa!

The home of varied species of animals

The sunny and worlds hottest continent

Best known for her breathtaking tourist attractions centers.

My Africa!

The home of beaches and islands

World heritage site, rich in cultural heritage and diversity

A wealth of natural resources

Home of languages, about 1500-2000

Languages are spoken in her territory

Source of the world's longest river

The world's second largest and second populous continent.

Home of great and productivity

People endowed with creativity

Industrious and hardworking.

Oh my Africa!

Home of natural resources

Her sons and daughters are out to grow

And build the world with her precious stones and glittering metals.

Home of literature and arts

Her sons and daughters have spread abroad

Showering glory on her name,

For her labour can't be in vain.

Home of pyramids and mountains

Beaches and islands

Her naturally endowed Beauty makes her exceptional

And a center of attractions for all.

AFRICAN PROVERBS

By Wilfred Ntui

The proverbial school of thoughts, the inspiring aged people, specifically our heroes, who's the moonlight spent time to write the African board their great inspiring quotes to liven the soul of the youngsters.

They taught us to make Hays while the sun keeps shining, to examine what is said, not who is speaking, and to look where we feel, but not where we slipped.

They warned us "saying" a man being short does not make him a boy, hot anger is not capable of cooking yams, and the same sun that melts the wax is also capable of hardening the clay.

And finally, they dropped their last words "saying" there are no shortcuts to the top of the palm tree, the waters of the river flow on without waiting for the thirsty man, and that no person is born great; great people become great when others are sleeping.

LET US GROW TOGETHER

By Wilfred Ntui

I'm a human not by the colour

Not by race but by my thinking capacity

This unique feature

Is only seen in humans, animals are exempted.

I'm an African not by intention

Nor choice but by God's wisdom

That surpasses cardinal analysis.

I'm a Nigerian not by awareness

Nor signatory but by the mystery of the womb designed from above

To fulfill a task undone.

Don't judge me by what my nationality is known for

But rather by what you noticed about me

With fairness, good conscience and moral virtue.

The mystery is unknown to all

But the fact remains that we all makeup the world

Yes! I mean me and you!

Buzz the world has none but me and you.

Let's strive for peace, unity and progress

With these we can make the world a better

A place for all.

TELL MAMA

By Uwaoma George Chinomnso

With hot tears rolling down my cheeks

Tears of agony; agony of my own death

Tears that were dried up even before streaming down my chin

I tell my tales; this is my ordeal with life

This is what I got as a Nigerian

I could hear faint voices, screams, shouts, and wails.

Ariara main market Aba was unnecessarily loud today. The market is always noisy but todays own were too much.

One would think that a ceremony was going on but alas, they were rejoicing the death of a criminal.

They were in great jubilation seeing the smoke from the burnt tyre moving high into the sky like Abel's burnt offering.

In my struggle with death, I could see faces; faces that I thought would help me.

Oh Nigeria, what drained our sense of love and peace? I could see a rare kind of unity. An evil kind of unity.

They were chanting "burn him! Burn him!" with one voice.

I am that criminal. I am that burnt offering. I am those ashes being swept away by the cleaners the following day.

In my blurry vision, I beheld 7 yr oid Nkem standing and gazing; hands akimbo and mouth agape

It pained me to see my own sister watch my death. If only she knew that it was my death, it was not an act.

If only someone can explain to the mob that am innocent. I stole the money yes, but am not a thief.

I did it for mama

I did it for Nma

The local herbalist said that mama has arthritis, she can't walk

Mama couldn't go out to sell,

I couldn't sell my *pure water,* it was raining heavily

I couldn't watch Nma starve, there was no food in the house

I couldn't watch mama die, there was no money either

I had to do something; I didn't mean to steal but I had to

I thought of going out to buy snacks and sell for profit but there was no money anywhere.

Mama suggested that I go to aunty Amaka in the next street. Aunty Amaka refused to give me anything even when I explained the state of things at home.

I went to the Mallam selling suya and he too refused to give me anything.

Life has not been this way all along. I grew up with papa, mama and Nma.

2 years ago, we lost papa. The government killed him.

Papa had a big timber shop in the market. He supplies building materials to many big agencies and we were living very big.

It all started with an evacuation letter from the government. The government used their big tractors to bring down all my fathers lifetime business.

It was a big blast to us but we were still living fine. Papa had many buildings and many tenants.

Everything was still okay until the government killed him. He went out that fateful morning for protest with his fellow business partners. They were still protesting to the government over their business and damaged goods. He went out that black Tuesday and never returned home. The government ordered security operatives to shoot them all. Papa was no more.

That was the day the tide of life was turned against us. The day fate stopped smiling at us.

After his funeral, papas' siblings rose and took everything papa had worked for all through his lifetime.

They took everything including mama's retail provision store.

That was how I became a beggar.

I was still wrapped in those thoughts when I heard Nma crying then it dawned on me that she was still hungry

Nma had to eat

Mama had to take proper medication

I had to do something very fast

I saw myself running out of the house under the rain

I went out with the rain only to find food

I didn't come to steal

I only took the money and bought food and drugs

I was going to return the balance from the purchase

The owner had more than enough

Yet I was returning his balance, little did I know that the old blind beggar saw me when I took it

Little did I know that he had raised alarm when I sneaked away

Little did I know that he was not blind after all; the mob didn't notice that

But now, I am burning.

I can see the old fat lady pouring more fuel into the fire, so she had something to spare all these

While and didn't give me anything despite all my pleas

I recall the fulcnizer telling me vividly that he has nothing to spare; so, he can donate two new

Tyres to roast this game

Yes, I am a game caught by fate; fate is the hunter

I could hear the fire crackling and rustling, my skin was roasting

I can see the black nylon roasting with me

The drugs and the food; they didn't take it anymore

The balance from the purchase; they needed it no more

Please help me and pass this message;

Tell mama, you didn't breed a thief

Tell mama, I didn't steal Pa Efu's money; I only wanted to buy food

Tell mama, I am sorry for the disgrace

Tell mama…

If only they could listen… But they won't

They are burning in their desire to see me die

I don't blame them; they weren't like that before. Many of them are victims of the evacuation.

The country changed them

Their poverty changed them

Their ignorance chained them

The government was not helping

The hoodlums around were not pitying

And hunger was still scorching

Please tell mama never to allow Nma go out alone. The street boys are rough.

Tell her that I kept her Udara fruit under the bamboo bed waiting for it to ripe.

And again, before I give up

Tell posterity, I am not a failure

Tell posterity, I died seeking for life

Tell posterity, I only bought food and drugs

Tell posterity, I didn't write off billions of naira to myself

Tell posterity, I died only because I am poor

Tell posterity, I was killed only because of food and drugs

Tell posterity, they didn't find a gun with me

Tell posterity, I was killed because I am an African

Tell posterity, 10-year-old Ebuka wrote his own epitaph.

This is my epitaph. Inscribe it in my father's tomb since I was never buried.

AFRICAN MAIDEN

By Uwaoma George Chinomnso

Oh, African maiden, your shape is firmer than the statue of liberty

Your skin shines darker and emits fragrance of pageantry

Your white teeth obsess me whenever you smile for a pleasantry

Saying that you are beautiful can only turn out to be derogatory

Indeed, you are a goddess

I've traveled from Asia to America

Resided in Europe and later voyaged to Antarctica

Yet none can compare your beauty my dear senorita

I had no other option than to return home to you my Africa

Indeed, you are a goddess

Your bosoms forming two domed shaped cupolas

Out of your breasts flows milk sweeter than the loya

You satisfy all; both the complete and the apodal

You don't discriminate, oh Africa my dear maiden

Indeed, you are a goddess

Whenever you speak, your soothing voice calms my troubled soul

Because it is calm, peaceful and melodious, it uplifts me so

The savor from your body is a healing to my malady, it saves me from Sheol

The riches of your exuberance, I cannot find in any other, even in Sheoul

Indeed, you are a goddess

Oh, sweet maiden, you are original, full of essence

Other maidens decorate themselves for beauty but end up an illusion

They think that they are beautiful but not in my vision

But you are naturally beautiful with no imitation

Indeed, you are a goddess

In you, the creator showed his full-time unique craftsmanship

You are exquisitely superior to others, the maker's masterpiece

Whenever you pass, the young men of the world do hide and peep

Because the radiance of your beauty makes their heart skip

Indeed, you are a goddess

WHEN

By Charles Mercy

The sun is thirsty

The earth is wailing

Many hearts are waiting

And smiles are fading.

All eyes are weeping

The dreams are dying

The souls are longing

As many minds are darken.

The stars are dimming

The time is shortened

Fela songs are on repeat

As the radio is never turned off

Oh, on sad lonely days

Our father's stories

Are never too old to be told

To the younger ones ears.

When will there be hope !?

DO REMEMBER ME.

By Charles Mercy

Amina.

When my soul stop living

Wake and keep living

Oh Darling, let your journey begin

For I have taken the load with me.

I left but not gone completely

She knows of my existence

Yet choose not to dwell in the resistance

That was in her heart.

Saying this is all pretence

That I'm playing a game of test on her

Why am I taking too long to wake up?

For how long I took, she could wait

Wait for me, her dream man

Yet in reality she knew, but refuses to accept that I was gone.

Amina

Your eyes was all I needed

To lighten up the candles on my candle night

Your smile is all I need now

To brighten up my grave

Even just the whispering of my name

Is enough for a tear drop in my grave.

Amina

A forever was what I promised

But I was gone too soon

So sorry I left you behind

To write of my death

I was your world, and you were mine

But Amie, your world crumbled when war took me away from you

The day duty calls, I had to obey.

And now!

It saddens my heart, to know that your world

Was shattered by a flying bullet at the civil war.

Oh Amina!

Do remember me

Remember to write of our love

Every day you think of me

Oh write from my heart

For my heart holds yours

Write of the music we made together

Write of the high note I made staring at you

For how beautiful you are was my chorus

And your smile making each line melodious

Together we were an album.

Oh Amina!

Put our love song on repeat

In remembrance of me

My love.

MOONLIT NIGHT

By Favour Amon Nle

Watching the moon as it unfolds

How big it has become

Round, as it is

Coming out in its full form

Light it produces as it sits comfortably

On father's roof

Oh, how beautiful a sight it is to behold.

Chirping of crickets

Cracking sounds of bamboo bed

All spicing the night

As they bring back sweet memories

Of me, or was it my days as a child?

Haven't I loved to watch the moon?

Awake at night.

Oh, how I saw the mystery lady in black apparel

An infant strapped to her back

As she splits wood in the full moon

Had we not gathered at the foot of the mighty tree?

Seated with folded legs, mouths busy

As they could only chant on a lit night

"Wise one, tell us stories."

The metallic sound of the gong

Simultaneously leads us to the open town square

As I leapt and shouted on top of my voice

In the middle of the night

While scampering away for safety

As we played hide-and-seek

Till one by one we retire to our huts.

CHRISTMAS, AGAIN

By Favour Amon Nle

It was on a Christmas Eve

My joy knew no bounds

Flashes of memories swept across my face

Filled with mixed feelings,

Overshadowed now with smiles

A clear picture of how I was then

Probably a 6, 5 or even 8 year old

Punching the air with excitement,

Leaping with joy

Would wear the oversized dresses,

No choices,

They were the only available.

Here comes the long-awaited Christmas day,

The atmosphere filled with merry

Steams from Cooking pot on fossil fuels,

As father complimented the dish,

By putting a knife on our chicken's throat

Wearing our best attires as we moved in the street

Retiring back to our homes,

Tired and happy

It's been over 20 years

I've left for the City

Coming back to replace the fresh air trees provide

With an air conditioner

Mother's fossil fuels with a cooking gas and stove

Smiles on father's face as he made an introduction of me

I have made them proud

Children cluster around me

Like ants in love with sugar

They didn't leave without a watered palm

I could see me once like them

I wish they could grow to this stage

And remember the good old days

SWEET YESTERDAY

By Favour Amon Nle

Out at night, we came to play

Moon in sight and food to stay

Calling to friends in joyful Glee

Come let's savor this present spice

Stories of heroes, myths and legends

Old grannies will tell why bent

Hopeful a lesson to guide us we'll learn

And in the future grow to be better men.

Along crooked paths, we'll toddle home

After a hassled day at school or farm

Contented only by the things we own

For nature always cursed an envious palm.

Old days of plenty, even beggars gave alms

The good old days when peace was a virtue

Alas those days are far gone causing harm

Because we bit the fingers which gave us food to chew

BLACK IS BEAUTIFUL

By Nzononye Ebube Godsglory

Her head beautified with braids

A natural crown of glory

Worn without frown but euphony

The pride of maids

Underneath soft silk

Is a breast of milk

A sight that makes many drools

The nest of a fool

Beads bound around coil waist

Like gold it glitters

A spark that glisters

A waist kept chaste

Her skin shines as the sun

Portraying the image she upholds

A beauty to behold

A comparison to none

Her voice echoes airy

In melodious tunes

Conveying messages

To sooth the souls of the despondent

She's black and beautiful

Beautiful and black she is

Portraying the image she upholds

A beauty to behold

AFRICA MY HOME

By Nzononye Ebube Godsglory

Africa my home

I have never known you

But your tales lingers in my mouth

The tales I'd pass on

Africa my Africa

Your sweat flows down my chin

The sweat of your work

The work of your slavery

Africa my home

I have never known you

But your blood flows in my vain

Your resplendent black blood

A sign of our lineage

Africa my Africa

Tell me again your slavery

Hands shackled to your aching back

Burning in the sun

Your only witness

Africa my home

Grandmother always sang to you a million times

The happy sad lyrics I wish I understood

Africa my Africa

Your slavery now bravely

Your children now at liberty

Liberty at last

SALUTE TO THE LION

By Nzononye Ebube Godsglory

Oh lion king of the forest

Oh lion huge as hill even in your stout posture

Oh lion brave but clumsy

Yet your prey sees you as superior

Oh lion king of the forest

Whose teeth are like shafts

Devouring subjects

Who wails out in hunger

Oh lion who commands with just a roar

A Terror to thy subject

Oh lion, thy claws shines as trample on your prey

As large as the elephant, it dare not speak against you

The creepy creatures shiver at thy footprint

A sign that you are near

Oh lion that ignore "We are hungry and jobless" let alone "There's no security"

Mountainous Animal

Huge beast with a heart of stone

Oh lion, when would that remember thy subject?

Who're now lean as stick

Oh lion king of the jungle

Oh lion wise and foolish

OCTOBER IST

By Nzononye Ebube Godsglory

Like flower she springs off

At her new age

The heart of her offspring

A beauty we long to stare at

Endowed with qualities

Yet veiled

The epitome of love

Now shattered

She's stain with red

Her wails lingers

Like dirge it's mourning

Soured Sweetness

A taste we now spit out

Her green now gray

Misused and polluted

Her blue now black

The thirsty earth has drank the whole water

Her dignity now punctured

Her worth now disregarded

She's a damsel in distress

She whimpers widely

But her offspring are deaf

She cleaves to the dimmest light

With hopes of restoration of her lost beauty

BALLAD

By Nzononye Ebube Godsglory

I sat to listen

As white hairs sang in unison

With aged voices gently gently

And eyes dancing in delight

I sat to listen

To the tales of my fathers

Who won victory over slavery

Saying no to the whip of the white man

I sat to listen

To the tales of my mothers

Who danced at river banks

Flaunting their pride as brides

I sat to listen

To a song so sweet

Stirring in me delight

With the moon as our only light

I sat to listen

As white hairs sang in unison

The song of my ancestors

Their slavery and victory

I sat to listen

MMAPULA THE RAIN QUEEN

BY Paulyn A Paolah

I wonder what happened

When they gave birth to me

A Dark Beauty African girl

It was the happiest day of my life

The day Nature blessed me

With amazing Beauty and great talent

While being held in warm hands

I wailed in a loud voice

In my nudity, I was shinning in Diamond

Showing the world that I have arrived

Proclaiming my very own birth

I am a Poet with a cultural Name

'Mmapula, the Rain Queen'

The world celebrated my birth

Birds of the Sky over whelmed with joy

As they await their Princess

Mmapula, the Poet.

Mmapula, the Rain Queen

Poor Mother carried me in her womb

Through that great pain, she found happiness

She gave me love and care

I was born naked

But she clothed me with culture

Raised me as an African lady with pride and dignity

And as a Rain Queen, I saw miracles all around

UBUNTU

BY Paulyn A Paolah

"I am because of you,

You are because of me"

Where is the spirit of Ubuntu?

Have we let it drawn beneath the waves?

There are so many empty arguments yet we lost our pride,

We are like slaves sinking in the tide,

Many are living in cages,

We are fighting in war of hunger,

Diminishing our intelligence,

Believing more in brutality than humanity,

Soldiers killing citizens,

Sons killing fathers, daughters killing mothers,

What Happened to UBUNTU?

The Ubuntu in Africa is falling like rotten leaves of a tree,

Our eternal love forgotten,

I desire the lost unity and shore of our kingdom,

Can't we form another great Pangaea?

Where is the simplicity of the act of kindness?

Where is our peace?

Why define each other by our color?

Why is our own slaughtered in daylight?

What happened to the spirit of Ubuntu?

Our dignity is swept,

No man is an island

Yet there are elites in our society

So called people of caliber descend on us like morning dew,

Our youths turned into Martyrs,

Each day is a massacre

Where is our Ubuntu?

I'm not a Kenyan,

Nor am I from the great land of Banyore,

I'm not a Tutsi nor am I a Xhosa

I'm an African,

Fighting to restore the spirit of Ubuntu,

To restore our spirit of togetherness,

Ubuntu!! Ubuntu

I am because you are

You are because I am.

UBUNTU

MOTHER CONTINENT

BY Paulyn A Paolah

I lack words to describe you; Mama Africa

Breathing the air of Africa is incredible

You cannot resist the lure of Africa

Affirmed with dark-skinned

What a shining colour!

What a glamour!

Mama Africa, Mother Continent

A home of magnificent creatures

Enormous mineral and fossil resources

Admirable culture and heritage

Our culture our identity

Our heritage our dignity

Mama Africa, Mother Continent

Full with captivating natural wonders

Dramatic coastline

Luscious Forests

Unforgettable architecture

Our beautiful Kilimanjaro

The great River Nile

Our alluring Lake Victoria

Our fertile grassland

Our animals

The pride of Africa

Mama Africa, Mother continent

Proud of our language

'Hakuna matata'

No worries

'sisi ni sawa'

We are the same

Mother continent you are angelic

Mama Africa you are dazzling

NYAR –YIMBO

BY Paulyn A Paolah

"A home without daughters is like a spring without a source,"

Born in the smoky hurt of Aketch

My nyar- yimbo

The beauty of a woman, yes daughter of soil

Her pekness , daughter from the great hills of Ramogi

Adoyo born in prowess

Back in the days of jorochere

Her beauty has been praised and sung by many nyatiti

She is a fleet as a gazzalle.

Did you see my Adoyo?

Her teeth has a bewitching gap

Her ears with earrings daggling from tiny holes

Her skin so dark like espresso

Her neck is like that of a whiskey bottle

Her tiny waist swaying beautiful

Oh her navel! Is like a pearl well located in her belle

Her chieno, well fitted in her body

Did you see her legs?

Were curved them out personally

Oh ! Adoyo the flying feet.

Did you see my Adoyo ?

The miaha

Mother to Obura

The physically fearless one

Whose first words were dwaro mara

Whose father great Gogni request thirty heads of cattle

Adoyo the centre of her father's eye

Have you ever set eyes on my Adoyo

SON OF MAMA AFRICA

By Adanu Michaels Fantasy

I am Oloche

A Grandson of Mother Earth

A true son of Mama Africa

From the Black-Gold skin of Mama Africa

I was pro-created

Inheriting both the heritage and culture

I am a child of the world

I am Oloche

A traditional man of the idoma Nation

Holding my cultures in high esteem

Standing in accordance with the Norms

Learning the story of Mama Africa

And teaching the values of my culture

I am a child of the world

I am Oloche

A descendant of Africa

The trumpeting voice of Rhapsody

A warrior of justice

A prophet of Ubuntu

The voice behind every page echoing 'Unity'

I am a child of the world

I am Oloche

That is what Mama Africa calls me

A true son of Africa

Fantasy, the wider world knows me with that

I am the poet with a vision of a united world

I am not just a son of Mama Africa

I am a child of the world

WAKING UP WITH AFRICA

By Adanu Michaels Fantasy

Africa my sweet mother

How proud I wake up every morn

With the thought of having a sweet mother as you

You bless my morning with joy

Extend the Noon with love

And night with peace

Every morning I spend time with Mother Africa

Tuning through the Radio people

Just to listen to the promising voice of Mother Africa

As she wakes her children with Morning blessings

I tuned to the Nigeria People

I feel the excitement as their tongue rolls

I enjoyed them all

The sounds of Ekaroo and Olodudu

The sounds of Inakwana and Unma'ochi

The sounds of Otutu'oma and Enale

They all bless my day with sweet melody

I tuned to South Africa, The Rainbow Nation

The same feeling of excitement serenade round

I enjoyed them all

The sounds of Molo and Unjani

The sounds of Thobela and Aweh

The sounds of Howzit and Dumela

They all flavour my morning with blissful colour

Then, breaking into my time with Mother Africa

Were the people of Aljazeera and BBC

What have they come with?

Another sad love song of misfortunes befalling the world

I broke down in tears as my heart wept

But standing by me was still Mother Africa

To heal and console me

My morning must not come with mourning

So I continued to tune through the Radio people

I found peace in the sounds of Asubuhi Nzuri and Habari Za asubuhi

Fate filled me with the sound of Maakye, Maa-ch and Akwaabe

These must be the loving people of Kenya and Ghana

They filled my day with peace

My heart was at a point of melt down

When the sounds of Bonjour and Mote serenade through my ears

Followed by the romantic sound of Naka subasi and Esama

These indeed must be the sweet voices from DR. Congo

And the lovely sounds from The Gambia

They set my morning for a fruitful day

Then I hear a tender voice

Sounding from deep within

From the outreach of my marrows

Of whom I was certain to be Mother Africa

And she said unto me

"Son, I have blessed your going out and coming in

Go and remember the Unity of Africa"

COME BACK MOTHER AFRICA

By Adanu Michaels Fantasy

Africa Oh Mother Africa

Come back oh mother Africa

Do not watch your children break away forever

Come back and unit us together

And teach us the true way of Africa

Africa Oh Mother Africa

You stand there ripped of your dignity

Like the Bride who lost her Groom at wedding Night

Blubbering over every single word

Like the re-sounding echo of an uncircumcised tongue

Come back and heal your home

Africa Oh Mother Africa

Your heart has been broken and shattered into pieces like a broken bottle

We have blind folded you in broad daylight

In other to execute our evil activities

We chased you away, so far away

In the name of Chrislam and Greekarab salvation

Come back with the true spirit of Ubuntu

Africa Oh Mother Africa

There you lay across the Nile

Weeping like a defeated Goliath

Lamenting like the desecrated man

Will you abandon your home forever?

Come back with a fight against immorality

And Re-claim your throne, true mother of Africa

Africa Oh Mother Africa

You hang up there in the sky

Watching every street covered with blood

Blood of your own children

In great distress you watch but you do nothing

Like a virgin girl raped of her dignity

You sober every word in terror

Come back and cleanse your home with the true blood of Africa

Africa Oh Mother Africa

We have seen how the mighty have fallen

We have seen earthquakes, firestorms and thunder strikes

We have seen troubles arising like the Blue Moon

We lament because we desecrated you

We are homeless because we broke your heart, our home

We are defenseless because we destroyed our shield

Come back and re-born your children with the true spirit of Africa

IDOMA CULTURE

By Adanu Michaels Fantasy

The golden talent of our generation

Here we are living the present for the future

Blessed by our fathers and passed unto us

And here we stand, making another future for the close future

As we celebrate the culture and tradition of our fathers.

The great inhabitants of the lower western Benue

A nation well known to be warriors, fishers and hunters of class

A nation who never turns away from her culture

"alekwu" the ancestral spirit of Idoma

"alekwu" the link between the living and the dead

"alekwu" the ancestor who usher showers of blessing upon us

A culture who teaches morality as a code of conduct

A culture with the symbol of peace, order and tranquillity

That culture is what I believe in

The Idoma culture

The red and black nation is a central cultural institute

At young age you teach your children the Idoma history by telling them folktales

Iduh, the father of Idoma, thy name is boldly written in our hearts

With the red and black culture handed down to us

This is indeed simple and a great nation

The people of Idoma, sons of Iduh

A fine culture they do have

I praise for the red and black nation

Green culture, green you were

After a revolt, after a red

You have added black

"ogirinya" the famous dance of Idoma

How beautiful they appear in red and black to display this dance

"ogirinya" a dance which requires jumping at interval

"ogirinya" a dance for only the healthy

This shows how healthy the red and black nation is

The red and black nation

Perhaps my blood is red and i write in black

Oh! my beloved Okoho soup

A soup whose aroma alone can relocate you from overseas

Have you had a taste of okoho and oni'hi or oni'be?

You could forget all your worries after a taste of idoma traditional dish

Prepared by our beautiful, loving and caring mothers

No wonder the annual food festival in Benue celebrates women and traditional cuisines

I believe in the red and black nation

We believe there is everything in Horoscope

We believe that all religion were basically the same

At least the one we read was

They all believe in love and goodness

They only matters on things of creation

Heaven, Hell, God, sin and Salvation

We believe in the red and black nation.

NOTES: Meaning of some terms

IDOMA*- a Nation in the North Central part of Nigeria, West Africa*

ALEKWU*- means an Ancestral spirit of the Idoma Nation*

IDUH*- the father of Idoma Nation*

OGIRINYA*- A famous dance in Idoma Nation*

OKOHO*- a traditional draw soup of Idoma Nation*

ONI'HI*- pounded yam and* ***ONI'BE****- black amala*

THE BROKEN HEART OF MOTHER AFRICA

By Adanu Michaels Fantasy

I hear hurling cries of sarcasm

Calling out against juvenile delinquency

I stirred in search of the caller with a hyperopic glare

Behold! Standing across the bridge was Mother Africa

Crying to bridge immoralities and restore the glory of African saga

I felt the broken heart of Mother Africa

Where have you hidden my pride?

There, stands Mother Africa questioning

Have you drown it in the debt of Nile or Niger?

Show me where you have taken it

That I may go and restore it

For Africa's pride I hold in high esteem

Where have the Mental Blinkers gone to?

Have you too been consumed by the storm?

Have your inks no power anymore?

There, stands Mother Africa in utmost dismay

Hoping to hear from the Army led by **Wole Soyinka**

The pride of Africa is what she seek

Those who have nothing but gun for the hungry

And think of nothing but death and dying

Let them spend their earth's fortune

Harvesting blood from the field of war

The last banquet shall be their children's children blood

There, stands Mother Africa in great lamentation

You have deserted the spirit of Africa

Africa has fled in shame from her home

You have invited immorality to be your god

With bad governments and corrupt leaders as its apostles

The just ones suffers injustice and the unjust go score free

There, stands Mother Africa weeping

I will remain at the River bank of Nile

Until you show remorse and repent

Until you are ready to embrace your culture

Until I see morality chase out immorality

When the court of mediocrity is broken, then I shall return

There, stands Mother Africa praying for her pride.

MAMA AFRICA

By Adanu Michaels Fantasy

I am Africa

One of the Seven Daughters of Nature

You can call me Mama Africa

Just like my Sisters, I grew up

My Dark skin could not even shadow my beauty

My sisters would always say "Africa is Black but Africa is Beauty"

My beauty attracted so many suitors

But my dream was for all, one

Ubuntu

So I got married to them all

To have a united family bound with true love

To my Husband in the North

I bore six lovely children

With names that will always be remembered

Sweet Egypt, Libya and Tunisia

Lovely Algeria, Morocco and Western Sahara

Their skin glows but still United to Mama Africa

To my Husband in the West

I bore eighteen children

Great children with great future

Dearly Benin, Burkina Faso, Cameroon, Cape Verde, Chad and Cote d'ivoire

Amazing Gambia, Ghana, Guinea, Guinea Bissau, Liberia and Mali

Beautiful Mauritania, Niger, Nigeria, Senegal, Sierra Lone and Togo

I taught them various language but still United to Mama Africa

To my Husband in Central Africa

I bore six children

They are the Heart of my home

My Angelic Central African Republic, Congo and Democratic Republic of Congo

My Peculiar Equatorial Guinea, Gabon and Sao Tome and Principe

They are the central unit of my home and still United to Mama Africa

To my Husband in the East

I bore fourteen children

Fourteen children with great vision

My Darling Eritrea, Ethiopia, Somalia and Djibouti

My Fabulous Sudan, Uganda, Kenya, Tanzania, Rwanda and Burundi

My Icing Comoros, Mauritius, the Seychelles and Madagascar

When you see the men from the East, they come in Swiss but still
United to Mama Africa

To my Husband in the South

I bore ten children

Children of Greater Africa

I take Pride in Angola, Botswana, Lesotho, Malawi and
Mozambique

I take confidence in Namibia, South Africa, Swaziland, Zambia
and Zimbabwe

No matter the distance, they are still united to Mama Africa

To all my children

I taught various cultures and languages

Not to create difference

But to harmonize the Beauty of African culture

Through Carnivals and cultural feasts

To show the world the unimaginable Beauty of Mama Africa

UBUNTU

By Adanu Michaels Fantasy

I am because you are

You are because I am

Ubuntu!

This is the fate of Mother Africa

Fore-told by her Beloved Arch-Bishop Desmond Tutu

Ubuntu!

This is the prayer of beloved Mother Africa for her Children

Have we suddenly gone deaf?

That we can no longer listen to the hurling cries of Mama Africa

Look! There she stands across her Homeland

With the shame of lost dignity or should I say pride

As she echo every silent whisper

"Where is the spirit of Ubuntu in my home?"

How do I dwell among your children?

Do you not see the streets covered with blood?

What about the established difference between the Rich and Poor?

The so called leaders now tear the society apart

I am black skinned but with a pure heart

My black is pure of gold not of rotten dead coal

There, standing far away is Ubuntu

Answering to Mother Africa with great lamentation

I am skin Black, you are White

This is not Ubuntu

I am Ghanaian, you are South African

This is not Ubuntu

My culture forbids, your culture tolerates

This is not Ubuntu

Ubuntu sees the white in every black skin

And the black in every white skin

Ubuntu thinks of Africa to the World

Not of Nation from Nations

Ubuntu teaches only one culture 'Unity'

I am because you are and you are because I am

Ubuntu!

This is where my pride lies

Without you there is no Africa

Without Africa there is no you

There is no future without forgiveness

Make your heart my home and I will come, bringing good tidings

Forgive they who wrong you

Unit they who are scattered

Restore my dignity and I will restore your peace

I am because you are

You are because I am

THE FATE OF UDEH By Adanu Ochanya Dorcas

THE FATE OF UDEH

Mr Udeh, a great farmer of his time lived in Iko and was married to three wives. The first wife (Onyeche) had no child, the second (Elameyi) had two female children (Ada and Olohi) and the third (Ajuma) had a son (Adole). The three wives had a good relationship with each other, they would help their husband in the farm, go to the market together most of the time and they would go to the stream together.

Mr. Udeh, the great farmer as his villagers would refer to him anytime he passed to the farm was a very generous man, he cultivates yam and grains with the help of his wives and two female children and he was a very hardworking and committed farmer who never lacked anything in his household.

The unity in Udeh's household became very strong to an extent that other villagers envied them. They wished they would have a taste of coming from such family; of course everybody wants to be happy but along the line something happened and Udeh lost the cheers in his household. He became a topic of discussion in the village and among his peers.

One day Elameyi, Udeh's second wife came out of her hut with Ada and Olohi, she went to the hut where her husband was sitting down and drinking palm wine, she greeted him and said "my husband I have come for us to make plans for our daughters to start schooling because they are five years behind. After saying this, Udeh looked at her from head to toe, looked at the children from head to toe, and he stood up, hissed and left them without saying a word. The girls stood in shock, they asked their mother what that was about but she could not say a word because she was confused. But on the other hand, Ajuma, Udeh's third wife, the mother of Adole had become the favorite because Udeh had sent her son to school and did everything for her, he even went as far as opening a shop for her in the market where she would be selling while the other wives go to the farm with their husband and children and as a result of this, Udeh's third wife had become too arrogant to her co-wives and she would treat the girls like salves. Udeh continued this for over a year, taking the girls to the farm and enslaving them, their mother would try to confront him but he would insult and beat her up. She would only cry and console the girls; the first wife felt pity for them and told them to be strong that everything would be alright.

The girls always wonder if Udeh was truly their biological father, they would cry and ask their mother but she forbid them from saying such. On a faithful evening, the girls' summoned courage to go and ask their father why he had refused to send them to school but the only thing Udeh said to them was "I cannot waste my money, time and resources sending you both to school because very soon, I will get you both married and you will be out of my life for good, girls are not meant to be educated. Education is meant for only boys who would in turn help their parents. Upon hearing these heart breaking words from their father, they cried all night.

The following morning, Udeh had asked the girls to go to the farm but they were tired because they had worked a lot at the farm the previous day. Ada said to her father "father please let us take rest today, by tomorrow I promise, I and my sister will finish the work"Udeh couldn't understand what his daughter just said so he said "do you mean you can't go to farm? And they said "yes father "Udeh sent them out of his house that morning after giving them the beating of their life. He said "I can't keep lazy animals in my house". He didn't even allow them to take anything, they have no any other option than to leave the house, they cried but that could not solve any problem. They had no place to go to, their mother only thought of going to the neighboring village where she was raised but the girls had refused. They insisted on rather going to a distant community where they would not be heard of ever again. They walked for miles and were very tired and hungry; they needed rest so they sat along a narrow path under a tree and eventually fell asleep.

They village which they now found their selves is known as Ojantele and it happened that the Queen of the village was taking a walk that evening along with her Royal guards. As they walked by, the sleeping girls caught her attention and she went to them, woke them from their slumber and questioned them what brought them to Ojantele and from where they had come. They could barely respond to any of her questions so she instructed the guards to help them up and immediately helped them to the palace.

The next morning they woke up in a big luxury house, the girls were shocked and couldn't figure out how they managed to enter such a house but it was not too long before the Queen sent for them to be brought before her and the King. The king asked what they were doing on the road all by themselves. Ada stood up and said "long live the king, this is our story" she narrated before the King and his wife what had happened to them and they both felt really bad for them. So he promised to educate them to any level they want to go, upon hearing this, they were filled with joy, they thanked the king and his generous wife and the Guards showed them back to their room.

On the other hand, Udeh and his beloved son had become cat and rat in the village. Adole had become very rascal, naughty and stupid, he would beat his mother and threaten to kill his father, he would rape any girl he sees on a narrow path, he goes to people's houses to steal goats and their belongings. This act continued for years, everyone became scared of him because he was a spoilt brat and he could do whatever pleases him. Udeh had become very poor and wretched because his son had sold everything he had including his house.

The first wife had left them to her father's house, she couldn't bear the disgrace, she didn't blame the boy, and it was Udeh's fault. He over pampered Adole, she would say to herself. She really felt bad for the girls but she always prayed for them.

Udeh had regretted everything he did in the past, he don't even know the where about of the girls and his wife, he had made enquiries around the neighboring villages, but nobody seemed to have seen them around. He just concluded that they may be dead by now because the Adole had threatened to find them and kill them. He wept all through the night.

By morning he had set out his farm tools and was getting ready when news came to him that his son had murdered a village chief and had been arrested. Udeh went unconscious upon hearing this and remained that way for two days. The day of Adole's judgment by the village elders, Udeh went to see his ungrateful son for the very last time before they pronounced him dead, he was actually sentenced to death by hanging, everyone was happy about this except Udeh.

The day of his execution, the girls had heard the news and insisted on going to Iko to see their step brother one last time so the king delegated two of his chiefs to go with them with some guards, the girls were very sad because their only brother would end up in a very shameful and disgraceful way. Their mother didn't want to set her eyes on Udeh again, she was much bitter; her friends consoled her and took her away from there.

On reaching the village palace, no one seemed to recognize the two girls, only Udeh who had already seen the resemblance, he quickly went on his knees, and he was ashamed of himself. The girls sighted their brother and went to him, he was also ashamed of himself, the kind of life he had chose for himself, he didn't expect all these to happen "I am very sorry he said to his sisters with tears rushing down his cheek, they began to cry along with him. When the new village chief pronounced his execution, the guard's had already grabbed him but when the king arrived, he gave orders for the boy to be released and they obeyed him. Udeh was shocked to the bone and couldn't believe it, he was happy about this but his only trouble at that moment was how to face his two daughters and their mother "would they ever forgive me? He said to himself, but they had nothing against him.

The girls narrated their story to the community, and everyone felt pity for them. Ada, first daughter was now a graduate with first class result from the prestigious university Ilorin and had also got married to the king's first son who is the heir to the throne of Ojantele community while the second daughter Olohi, graduated from the same university and works in the biggest hospital in the Region as a Medical Doctor. All thanks to the king of Ojantele and his generous Queen who made all this happen.

Udeh was amazed at their narrations, he thought girls were useless and do not need education, but he have seen that he was ignorant about that. He was very sorry, he pleaded and they forgave him and accepted him as their father.

The king stood up and gave a wonderful speech, about the need of girl child education in Africa, he concluded by saying "female and male children are blessings from God, it is very wrong to maltreat female children, treat them equally for you can never tell what tomorrow has in store for them, God is the maker of all things in the world.

They all went home as one big happy family.

MIDNIGHT TALES By Nzononye Ebube Godsglory

MIDNIGHT TALES

"Kamsi, put out the electric light and bring the lamp here" mama said, she had always preferred lamplight to electric bulb, to her it was what made night tales exception. "Let do it just like our mothers did" she would always say whenever I asked about the lamp. She was dressed in white linen tonight, the darkness blended with her dark skin. "Kids gather around, I have a new story tonight" she beamed "Mommy we've ran out of diesel" I said frowning, I had been anticipating this night, where I got to hear another story from her. "No dear, there is diesel. Go and check my room, I bought some today" Almost remembering something she added "But! be cautious, you know it's dark in there" since my father died 11 months ago, mother embraced the dark, there wasn't an electric bulb nor candle light, it was creepy though but I guess she was still hurting. Few seconds later I was back, I watched keenly as she refilled the lamp and it glowed luminously.

A lot of kids came tonight, I wasn't surprised since we just vacated, and parents had no problem letting their kids out. We all sat in on our mats, the moon smiled down at us and the night insects sang in beautiful harmony. "Children I'm elated to see you all today, can someone remind me where we stopped last time" "Mama you finished the story last time, tonight you're going to tell us a new one" Nkem said, he sat across me in class. I've always had a crush on him but mother said it was too early for an eleven year girl to have a crush on a boy. There was absolutely nothing to dislike about him, he was brave, and neat, but he was smarter than I was, I guessed maybe because he was three years older.

"Thank you my son, tonight's story is about keeping chaste" mommy's voice brought me back to reality "my mother always told me this story, which was passed to her from my grandmother and that's what I'm going to tell you all tonight" and she began, her voice echoing in the dark.

* * * * * * * * * * * * * *

Oma was betrothed to Chinedu, her husband when they were kids and their relationship as teenagers was envious, they showed it wherever they went, in the river bank, the farmlands, on the lonely part that lead to the village market even in the market place. They loved each other very much to the extent parents used them as examples to their younger children who went against betrothal.

When Oma turned eighteen and Chinedu twenty-two they got married and started a life together, for ten years Oma was unable to bear a child, they became the talk of town. Any small gathering of woman probably had Oma as their topic of discussion; she became a known name in everybody's lips. "Why can't I have a child" She cried one night in Chinedu's arms" whom have I wronged, what did I do wrong" she lamented as hot tears rolled down her chin "Nne is alright, you've wrong no one ok" Chinedu said cuddling her warmly "God will give us children when it's time, dry your tears, you know I hate seeing you cry over this" "I don't have a choice, do I?" she asked with her teary eyes staring back at him "People are saying I aborted all my children or eaten them, they think I'm a witch! Or I had many lovers. And you know you're the only I had and will ever have. I'm tired ....I just tired" "Yes! I know and I also know that you aren't a witch, you've got to be patient with God" that night they both wept, holding on to each other for strength and support.

People change and so did Chinedu, after few more months, he started drinking, just to escape the mockery. His age mates jeered he was not man enough; he was referred to as an impotent man. The public humiliation was too much to bear and he found solace in drinking, he became a drunk and most times pour out his resentment on Oma. Day by day, his love for her began to fade but Oma continued trusting God for a child. When it seemed like she was about to fall in faith, a miracle happened, she took in and that alone brought a transformation.

Chinedu went on his knees and apologized for his ill manners toward her and their love was renewed again, and when she was delivered of her baby, it was a boy and they named him Okiki. He was the bravest hunter who ever lived and most handsome too, the wait was forgotten as all those who mocked them rejoiced with them. After Okiki, they had three more children who did beautifully well in their field too.

* * * * * * * * * * * * * *

" So you see kids, being patience would always pay, no matter how long we wait, there's always light at the end of the tunnel" Oge smiled looking at the beautiful eyes of the children around her" So who can tell me what he/she learnt tonight" she asked

"I learnt that patience pays" the youngest of us answered

"I learnt that we should apologize whenever we're wrong. Chinedu apologized to his wife and their love grew stronger". Few more replies came and within few minutes mom concluded and they all went home anticipating the next eke night to listen to mama's sweet folktales.

"Mom?" I came closer to her " I love tonight's story, it was tragic though especially the part where Oma had to wait 10 years for Okiki, but she smiled that last" "Kamsi, you should know that life isn't a bed of roses, we have sad times too but we need to hold on to God for strength" she said putting her arms around me "Now let's go in, it's late, tomorrow is another day".

Contributing Authors Profile

1. **BABANGIDA B. SHIRA**

About the Poet

Babangida B. Shira was born in the Republic of Nigeria, Bauchi state, Shira LGA.He is a poet, bibliophile,literary analyst, essayist, co-authored: A Selection of Literature and Poetry with Ukiyoto Publishing Company, Canada.

1. **WILLIAM WARIGON**

ABOUT THE AUTHOR

William Warigon is an indefatigable Nigerian Legal practitioner and prolific writer from Demsa,Adamawa state. He lives in the aesthetic city of Abuja and loves reading, writing and discussing topical issuers.

1. **SUNDAY MATTHEW EDEH**

Born on November 9th, 1997 into the family of Mr and Mrs Ijeh Matthew. Sunday Matthew Edeh hails from Utonkon district of Ado Local Government area of Benue State Nigeria. Known for this magical and outstanding display in playing with words, he came up with a quote "Knowing yourself is the best gift anyone can offer to himself".

He is a Poet whose poetic prowess and ability have grown beyond boundaries. To him the beauty of poetry is in the simplicity of its wordings. He is the proud Author of "Lily of the Nile" a collection of soul swallowing poems, which expresses the godliness and values in the feminine gender. It is filled with the fragrance of love and virtue. It is tossed with the beauty of love, happiness and romance. Lily of the Nile encompasses 28 savouring heartfelt poetic expressions published by Love of a poet.

4. **VICTOR CHINAZAEKPERE**

Victor chinazaekpere is a student of federal polytechnic Nekede in owerri, Imo State Nigeria where he is studying Electronical engineering in his 100 level. He is a writer, also known as the pen addict. Due to his love for writing, he enrolled with the GRACE INSPIRED STORIES and also other writing platforms were he won different certificate awards as best writer. He is also a graphics designer, a lover of music, an artist and a professional reader who won the 2019 readership competition during his tender age.

Victor chinazaekpere is student, a passionate writer who loves to impact lives with his writing skills.

5. **OLETU OGHENENYORE CORNELIUS**

OLETU OGHENENYORE CORNELIUS, is a native of Urhobo from Ughelli-South LGA of Delta State. He is a photographer and G.M.P. fabricator. A passionate poet and story-teller with over 500 poems on various themes, some publish in online book and magazine. You can reach him on +238140727762. Facebook: OLETU OGHENENYORE CORNELIUS PETR. His Facebook and Instagram poetry page is NYORE NOTE.

6. **WILFRED NTUI**

Wilfred Ntui hails from Akamkpa L. G. A. of Cross River State, Nigeria he is a true lover of poetry. He is currently pursuing a degree in political science and public administration in one of the most competing university in Nigeria. He has competed in so many contest internationally from different prestigious poetry groups online, and has also won numerous awards with them, among which are ; poet of the week, best award of excellence, best international guest award to mention but a few. His earnest desire to improve the world around him through the use of pen knows no bound; he's so enthusiastic in his writing career and hopes to become a motivational speaker in the nearest future.

7. **UWAOMA GEORGE CHINOMNSO**

Uwaoma George Chinomnso is a student of Biology science at Alex Ekwueme federal University Ndufu Alike Ikwo, in Ebonyi state, Nigeria. He is a native of Ntalakwu Oboro in Ikwuano Local Government Area Abia State. His love for literary works drove him into writing poems and stories despite being a science student and have written lots of poems and stories.

Outside his academic pursuit, he is also into photography, videographer and editing.

8. **CHARLES MERCY**

Charles Mercy, A 200 level medical student of federal university lafia, Nasarawa state.

I love poetry, I write stories, content and poems. Looking forward to be a great writer, I guess its in me already.

9. **Favour Amon Nle**

Favour Amon Nle is a young poetess based in Rivers State, Nigeria. She is a content creator, a storyteller and an aspiring to be a lawyer. Yet to publish but something is cooking. She can be reached via Facebook @Favour Amon Nle.

10. **ADANU OCHANYA DORCAS**

Adanu Ochanya Dorcas, was born on 21st day of September, in the year 2001, in Ogobia-Ugboju, Benue State Nigeria, to the family of Mr. and Mrs. Adanu Ogwiji James, who hailed from Aukpa-Adoka of Otukpo L.G.A in Benue State. Attended St. Benedette's Nursery & Primary School from 2008-2013, continued my Secondary Education in St. Mary's College Ondo Ugboju from 2014-2019.

I obtained a degree in Data Processing from Andysyncline Computers Ogobia-Ugboju in the year 2019 and hoping to pursue my Tertiary Education soon.

11. NZONONYE EBUBE GODSGLORY

NZONONYE EBUBE GODSGLORY born on 7 December, 2003 to the famiy of Mr. and Mrs. Nzononye in the rural community of Umunede and brought up in Asaba, Delta state Nigeria where I had my secondary school education and graduated 2020. I dived into the writing journey in 2019 and it has been a great experience since then.

d

12. PAULYN A. PAOLAH

Paulyn A. Paolah, (Psychopen) Born on 17th January 2001, into the family of Mr. and Mrs. Juma an eagle based in Busia Kenya. A poet who is adorned with playing skillfully with words in the raisin 'dawn cripples herself with manacles of rhymes and rhythms enchaining the hearts of the tyrants. I am a Novelist and have participated in poetry contest at different levels. I believe poetry is when an emotion has found its thought and the thought has found words, it is a language that is more distilled and most powerful. My unlimited perfection shines. I'm pursuing English Literature and Information Science currently on my second year.

13. **RUTH KOECH JEPKORIR**

I am twenty years old. Koech Jepkorir Ruth from strikingly beautiful country Kenya. I reflect a varied personality including ambition, and the qualities of generosity and thoughtfulness. I am also a well determined and vigorous individual, yet pleasantly calm. I encourage fighting for what you desire and believe in, and doing it through God because nothing great comes easy and with God everything is possible.

I am a full-time student, motivated by my love for learning and succeeding as I strive to become an outstanding and successful woman in today's society. With the definitive goal of becoming a professional poet, I am currently starting Bachelor degree program in English literature at Kisii University Main Campus Kenya and am the senior member of the art and poetry club.

14. **EZENWAJIAKU ADAEZE PEARL**

EZENWAJIAKU ADAEZE PEARL hails from Anambara state, Nigeria and was born on the 24th day of November, 2008. She is currently in senior secondary school at African Child College, Abuja Nigeria

15. **PRECIOUS LAWRENCE**

Precious Lawrence hails from Abia state, Nigeria

CONTRIBUTING AUTHOR'S EMAIL CONTACT ADDRESS

BABANGIDA B. SHIRA- babangidababashira@gmail.com

WILLIAM WARIGON - williswarigon@gmail.com

SUNDAY MATTHEW EDEH- edehmatthew48@gmail.com

VICTOR CHINAZAEKPERE-victorchinazaekpere208@gmail.com

OLETU OGHENENYORE CORNELIUS-oletucornelius@gmail.com

WILFRED NTUI-wilfredntui@gmail.com

UWAOMA GEORGE CHINOMNSO-georgekennschino@gmail.com

CHARLES MERCY-charlesmercyidmudia@gmail.com

Favour Amon Nle-akarafavourmonday@gmail.com

ADANU OCHANYA DORCAS-adanudorcas53@gmail.com

NZONONYE EBUBE GODSGLORY- nzononyegodsglory@gmail.com

PAULYN A. PAOLAH- paulineapiyo2018@gmail.com

RUTH KOECH JEPKORIR- ruthkoech749@gmail.com

EZENWAJIAKU ADAEZE PEARL- ojukwucynthia1@gmail.com

PRECIOUS LAWRENCE-preshyvibes@gmail.com

ADANU MICHAELS- adanumichaels900@gmail.com

Author's Biography

ABOUT THE AUTHOR

Adanu Michaels (fantasy) born on November 2nd, 1997 to the family of Mr. And Mrs. Adanu. Born and brought up in the rural community of Ogobia-ugboju district of Otupko Local Government area of Benue State, Nigeria. Fantasy as popularly known grew up with lots of mixed development and experiences which contributed to majority of my poems focusing on the theme "Lamentations"

As at 2020, I could only boast of a secondary school certificate and a further Advanced level in education. My first publication was a collection of Poetry Titled "Trumpet of Rhapsody" This was published by ukiyoto publishing house and it is available on Amazon. Trumpet of Rhapsody cut across poems on Nature, culture, Dirge, Lamentations, Birthdays, fantasies, love and others. This is a collection where I blend both ancient and modern poetry to bring out the beautiful nature of literature ranging from the beauty of African cultures and traditions to love, Romance as well as fantasies and most importantly, discusses the ungodly circumstances through my poems on lamentations.

I also had the opportunity to contribute to the anthology "sweet sounds of poetry" by award winning Author Tamikio Dooley and co-author the anthology book "Art of Literature" with Author Tamikio Dooley also. I have participated in poetry contest at different levels

One thing I believe is "the world is being moved negatively %90 by people who think there is nothing else to be done" why not join the few voices who still believe in building a better generation

About The Book

ABOUT THE BOOK

The book African child anthology is a collection of poems and short stories circling around the cultures, traditions and ethics of the African Nation. It attracts writers from various African countries with the common idea of unifying Africa and teaching the African cultures and traditions not just to the young generation of Africans but also beyond Africa to the wider world

Some writers in this anthology points out the current situations in their respective African countries and provides possible ways of curbing these ill fate which befalls the Nation. Other contributing Authors bring out in this collection the beauty of the African culture and tradition.

Printed by Libri Plureos GmbH in Hamburg, Germany